Adding 1

- Count the stars.

  How many are there altogether?

  Trace the number.

and   makes   2

- Finish the sum.

1 + 1 = ☐

- Draw 1 more spider.

Adding 1

● How many balloons are there in total?
Count them all and trace the number.

● Finish the sum.

● Count the cupcakes.
Draw 1 more.
How many now?

Adding 1

- How many birds are there in total?
  Count them all and trace the number.

   and  makes

- Finish the sum.

3 + 1 =

- Count the worms.
  Draw 1 more.
  How many now?

Adding 1

● Count the sweets.

How many are there altogether?

Trace the number.

and   makes   5

● Finish the sum.

4 + 1 =

● Draw 1 more orange.

How many are there now?

Adding 2

- Count the fish.

  How many are there altogether?

  Trace the number.

and   makes   2

- Finish the sum.

$$0 + 2 = \boxed{}$$

- What is 2 more than 0?

  Circle the right number.

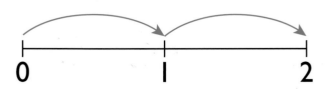

2

0   I

Adding 2

- How many pencils are there in total?
  Count them all and trace the number.

 and makes 3

- Finish the sum.

1 + 2 = ☐

- Draw 2 more balls.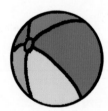

Adding 2

- How many monkeys are there in total?
  Count them all and trace the number.

and   makes   4

- Finish the sum.

2 + 2 =

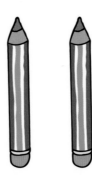

- Draw 2 more pencils.

Adding 2

- Count the apples.
  How many are there altogether?
  Trace the number.

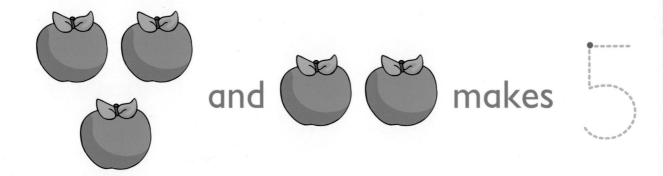

and makes

- Finish the sum.

$$3 + 2 =$$

- Draw 2 more kites to make a total of 5.

Adding 3

- Count the cakes.

  How many are there altogether?

  Trace the number.

and ... makes 3

- Finish the sum.

$$0 + 3 = \boxed{}$$

- Write the total number of spots on the dominoes.

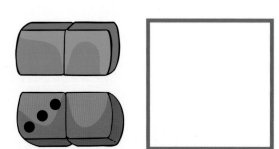

Adding 3

● How many lollies are there in total?

Count them all and trace the number.

and ... makes ... 4

● Finish the sum.

$$1 + 3 = \boxed{}$$

● Draw more flowers to make 4 altogether.

Adding 3

- How many rugby balls are there in total?
  Count them all and trace the number.

 and makes 5

- Finish the sum.

$$2 + 3 = \boxed{}$$

- Draw more balls to make 5 altogether.

Adding 4

- Count the candles.
  How many are there altogether?
  Trace the number.

and   makes   4

- Finish the sum.

  0 + 4 = ⬜

- Draw some balloons
  to make 4 altogether.

Adding 4

- Count the foxes.

  How many are there altogether?

  Trace the number.

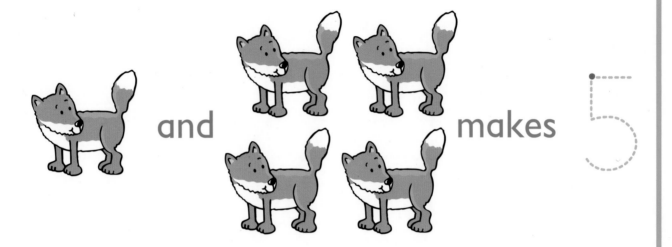

and makes 5

- Finish the sum.

$$1 + 4 =$$

- How many more do you need to make 5?

Adding 5

- How many sandwiches are there in total?
  Count them all and trace the number.

and makes 5

- Finish the sum.

0 + 5 =

- Count the fingers.
  Write the number.

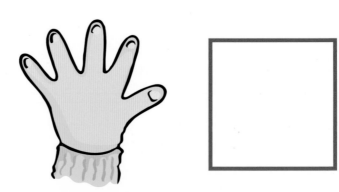

Take away

- Cross out 0 apples to find the answer.

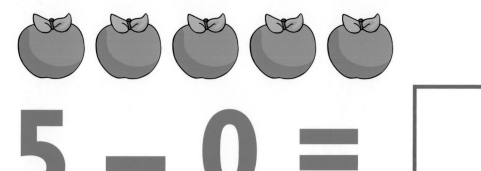

5 – 0 =

- Cross out 1 pear to find the answer.

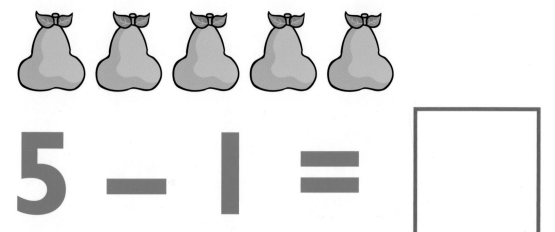

5 – 1 =

- Cross out 2 oranges to find the answer.

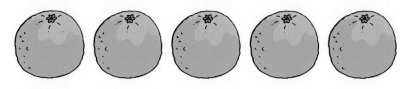

5 – 2 =

Take away

- Cross out 3 strawberries to find the answer.

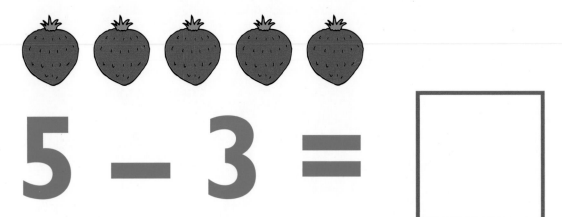

5 – 3 =

- Cross out 4 lemons to find the answer.

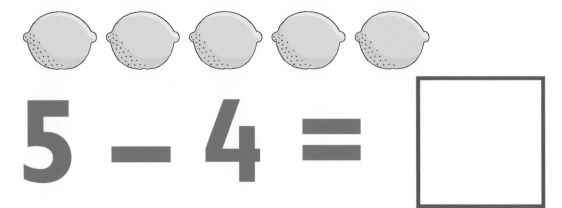

5 – 4 =

- Cross out 5 coconuts to find the answer.

5 – 5 =

Number facts to 5

- Count all the cubes and trace the answer.
  Then finish the number sentence.

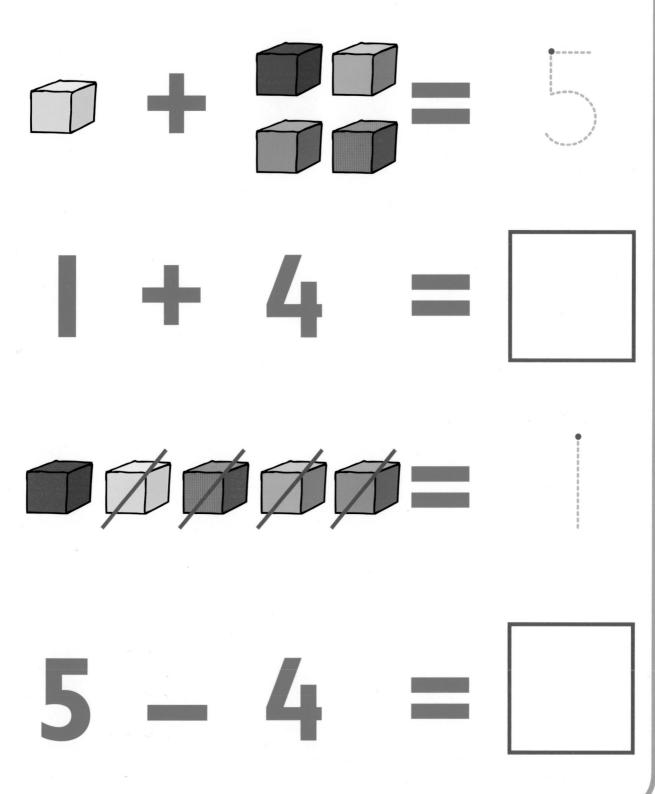

$$1 + 4 = \boxed{}$$

$$5 - 4 = \boxed{}$$

Number facts to 5

● Count all the cubes and trace the answer.
Then finish the number sentence.

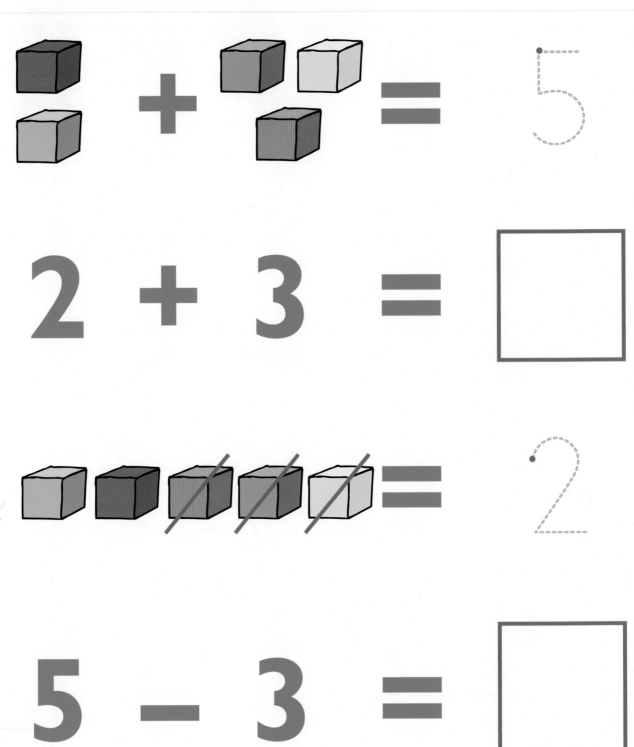

$2 + 3 =$

$5 - 3 =$

20

Number facts to 5

- Count all the cubes and trace the answer.
  Then finish the number sentence.

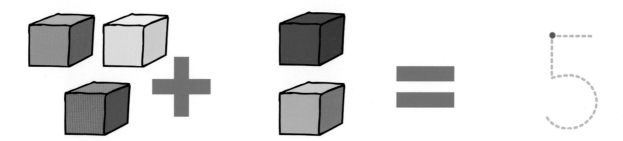 = 5

3 + 2 = ☐

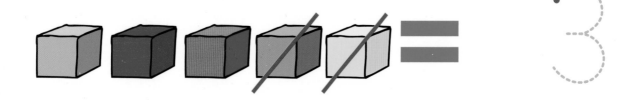 = 3

5 − 2 = ☐

Number facts to 5

- Count all the cubes and trace the answer.

  Then finish the number sentence.

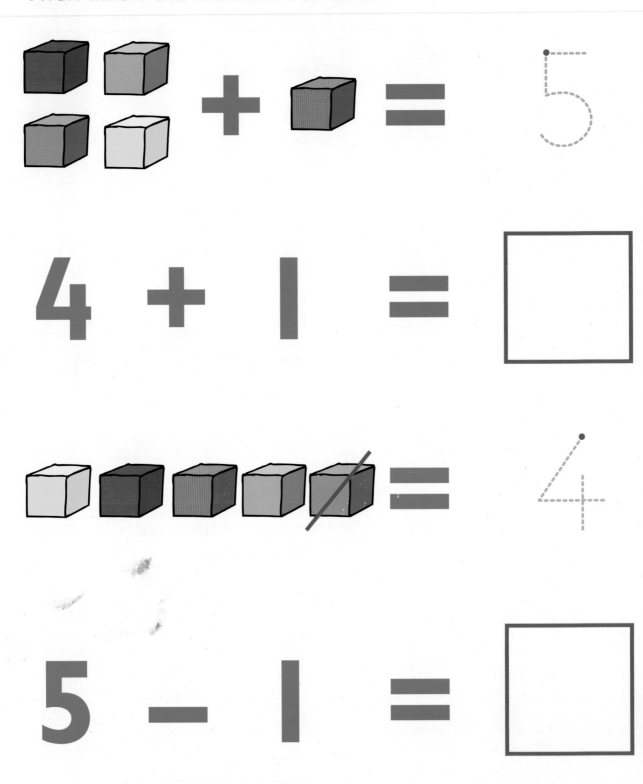

$$4 + 1 = \boxed{}$$

$$5 - 1 = \boxed{}$$